T0266651

Little Books on Liturgy

Samuel Torvend, series editor

Also in the series:

SAMUEL TORVEND

FOR THE LIFE OF THE WORLD

THE ESSENTIALS OF EPISCOPAL WORSHIP

SAMUEL TORVEND

FOR THE LIFE OF THE WORLD

THE ESSENTIALS OF EPISCOPAL WORSHIP

A little book on liturgy

CHURCH
PUBLISHING
INCORPORATED

Church Publishing Incorporated
19 East 34th Street
New York, NY 10016

Cover design by Jennifer Kopec, 2Pug Design
Typeset by Progressive Publishing Services

Library of Congress Cataloging-in-Publication Data
A record of this book is available from the Library of Congress.

ISBN-13: 978-1-64065-418-1 (paperback)
ISBN-13: 978-1-64065-419-8 (ebook)

Contents

Introduction

There is a risk in suggesting that something may be essential in life or in faith. Inevitably, someone will say, "You forgot this" or "You overlooked that." What might be essential for this person's life or this community's gathering may not be so for others. And yet we know some things *are* essential for life: air to breathe, food and drink to nourish, shelter and clothing to protect from the elements, rest as well as movement, companionship in some form, and care for the well-being of bodies and souls. From time immemorial, human beings have sought the essentials that enable life to flourish. If they weren't essential, would we need the enormous energy expended in responding to the contemporary reality of pollution, food insecurity, water privatization, child poverty, homelessness, and inadequate healthcare?

Is it possible to say the same regarding worship—that there are essentials? Since the nineteenth century, Episcopalians and Anglicans have sought to find what we have in common with other Christians rather than focus on all that separated us from each other in the eighteenth century (Methodism), in the sixteenth century (Catholicism and various forms of Protestantism), in the eleventh century (Eastern Orthodoxy), and in the fifth century (Oriental Orthodoxy). While centuries of conflict kept Christians of different communions from speaking with each other, the past century has revealed a shared pattern of worship beneath the distinctive elements and, within that pattern, common elements.

The Episcopal *Book of Occasional Services 2018* points to these common elements when it states, "It is important to maintain the centrality of the essential symbols for the assembly: font, word, and table" (*Book of Occasional Services* 18). Note that the directive does not say optional, occasional, or arbitrary symbols but rather "essential" symbols.

We would be remiss, however, if we left it at that, and gave the impression that a church directive should be accepted at face value without question, a kind of instructional dogmatism. Rather, these four elements—the assembly of those gathered, the word, the font, and the table—speak more of actions than unmoving things that one might find in a churchy museum. The *people gather* and become an assembly; *the Word of God is proclaimed* by members of the assembly with responses from the gathered congregation followed by an interpretation of this word leading to prayer for the church and the world; at times there is *a washing in water and the Name of God* with prayer, anointing, and welcome by the assembly; *thanksgiving over bread and wine* at the eucharistic table is offered by the presider with the assembly singing, acclaiming, and confirming the thanksgiving; there is then *eating and drinking* that leads to a dismissal into the world. Assembly, word, font, and table do not describe immovable, sacred objects but rather the central and life-giving sources of a living organism, an ensemble of actions with words that bestow and nourish Christian identity and set forth the purpose, the mission of this assembly.

The thoughtful person might ask, "Why are they called essential?" In a consumerist culture that demands seemingly endless options, to suggest that something may be essential may be construed as limiting choice. And yet we rightly remember the close relationship between life and liturgy: Birth in the watery womb brings us into a household; food and drink nourish life and living; a sense of belonging is made possible through gestures, movements, words, and clothing. That is, the very actions that many associate with "church" have their origin in the household, in the essentials needed to live. Perhaps this is why in their efforts to describe the community that emerged from the life, death, and resurrection of Jesus Christ, the writers of the New Testament use the terms "household" or "companions on the way."

But there is more: it is through the "essential symbols" that we encounter the One who comes to the assembly. Early and medieval Christians grasped artistically the advent of the triune God to the people of God assembled for worship: Above and behind the altar, an image of Christ was painted or created with mosaic, a nimbus or halo of the Spirit's energy surrounding Christ's body, and God's hand holding a laurel wreath of victory hovering above Christ's image. What did the artists portray? The advance or advent of Christ to *this* assembly gathered around the proclamation of the Word of God, the water washing called baptism, and the sharing of bread and wine cup called the Eucharist. It was and it is through these essential things, these very ordinary and earthy things, that the assembly encounters the wounded and risen Christ who gathers, who speaks in our midst today, who washes seekers into his body, who gives himself away as food and drink, and who leads the assembly forth into the world.

In this little primer on the essentials of worship, we hope to describe this vibrant center of Anglican worship, with its ecumenical gifts, for the life of the world. While the North American past witnessed a church governed by the state (the Church of England) and a church frequently allied with cultural privilege (the Protestant Episcopal Church in the United States), the assumption that people will be attracted to such established institutions no longer holds, if it ever did. The assumption that spiritual seekers in an increasingly secularized society will be attracted to a church because of its musical heritage, its cherished traditions, an open welcome, or its open-mindedness no longer holds—though all of these are much-loved marks of Anglican spirituality. Why claim that such assumptions no longer hold? They participate in a way of thinking about Christian faith and life that sounds much like this: "If we build it, they will come." Or this: "We expect you, the seeking soul, to come to us."

In July 2018, the General Convention of the Episcopal Church approved Resolution A068, a resolution that initiated the process of liturgical and prayer book reform. That same resolution highlighted something new: it placed worship and the reform of worship in the service of "God's mission . . . of loving, liberating, life-giving reconciliation and care for creation." Rather than begin with the notion that the primary purpose of worship is to get people through the door of the church, it suggested the opposite: One of the primary purposes of worship is to invite the gathered assembly to participate in the advance of God *into the world*. As the Eastern Orthodox Church has long said, the church's liturgy leads to the liturgy in the world: the service and witness of the people of God in daily life.

That same resolution highlighted these concerns: the language of worship will be marked by the riches of scripture and an expansive use of images; the liturgy will animate and serve the loving, liberating, and life-giving mission of the triune God; the patterns of worship will be faithful to the historic rites of the church, among them baptism and Eucharist; and the church's liturgies will uphold this church's commitment to care for the creation in a time of global climate change. The outline of this book reflects these concerns. Chapter 1 focuses on the primary language of Christian faith and life: on story, ritual, and symbol and the power of the primary language of scripture to offer a vision of life that enriches and transforms human experience. Chapter 2 sets forth the mission of God as revealed in the life, death, and resurrection of Jesus, a mission that took place in public and invites the contemporary assembly into that public mission. Chapter 3 unfolds the meaning of initiation into the Christian community and asks the reader to consider how baptism and its annual renewal among the baptized is guided and even challenged by a loving, liberating, and life-giving mission. Chapter 4 explores the origins of what may be called the historic shape of worship on the LORD's Day, Sunday: its origins, its continuity amid change, and its purposes. And finally, chapter 5 invites the reader to consider how worship on Sunday, prayer during the week, and the seasons of the year inform an ethic of care for God's creation.

By virtue of its length, something will inevitably be left out. But wait! This is only the first of eight small books on the liturgy.

There is more to come in this series, inviting readers and groups gathered for discussion to consider why reform is an ongoing task for any community engaged with the larger world. That larger world is the object of God's love and mercy revealed in Jesus Christ, a love that animates the transformation of our affections and our commitments to the common good. Embrace, then, these reflections on living together for the life of God's world.

Questions for Discussion

1. If you were to make a list of what is essential in your life, what would be the top five essentials? Why do you choose these five?

2. When you reflect on your experience of worship in your parish, what do you consider essential? Why?

3. When have you experienced the need for change or reform in your life? What prompted this awareness? What happened?

4. What would be one change in worship you would promote? Why is it important to you?

1 ▪ The Language of the Liturgy Is Scriptural

Moses was keeping the flock of his father-in-law Jethro, the priest of Midian; he led his flock beyond the wilderness, and came to Horeb, the mountain of God. There the angel of the LORD appeared to him in a flame of fire out of a bush; he looked, and the bush was blazing; yet it was not consumed. Then Moses said, "I must turn aside and look at this great sight, and see why the bush is not burned up." When the LORD saw that he had turned aside to see, God called to him out of the bush, "Moses, Moses!" And he said, "Here I am." Then he said, "Come no closer! Remove the sandals from your feet, for the place on which you are standing is holy ground."

Then the LORD said, "I have observed the misery of my people who are in Egypt; I have heard their cry on account of their taskmasters. Indeed, I know their sufferings, and I have come down to deliver them from the Egyptians . . . So come, I will send you to Pharaoh to bring my people, the Israelites, out of Egypt." But Moses said, "Who am I that I should go to Pharaoh, and bring the Israelites out of Egypt?" He said, "I will be with you . . . ."

(Exod. 3:1–5, 7–8, 10–12)

As a child in church school, I was taught to memorize the books of the Bible as presented in its table of contents. Of course, the first word out of my mouth when asked to recite the first five books was "Genesis." For the longest time I assumed that Genesis was the earliest memory of the Jewish people because it was about *origins*, in fact, two very different origin stories—Genesis 1:1–2:4a and Genesis 2:4b–25. It was only later in a college course on the Hebrew scriptures that I learned Genesis was not the first memory written by the authors of the Bible but rather it was the painful and joyous memory of enslavement in Egypt and the liberation of the Hebrew people from that imperial kingdom—its own kind of creation story: God giving birth to a free people, a new creation. That earliest memory of the Hebrews begins with enslavement, their cry to the God of their ancestors, and the odd encounter of Moses with a burning bush at Mount Horeb.

Perhaps the skeptic in each of us might wonder how a bush could burn yet not be consumed by fire. An argument over the factual nature of the story—arguments that have marked the history of Judaism and Christianity—will quickly distract from the larger and more significant movement within the story. Moses is attracted by the fire and comes close to it out of sheer curiosity. Yet what he encounters is the presence and the voice of God. This should not surprise us, as fire and light have been frequently associated with the presence of the numinous, the holy, the divine across cultures and religions. Indeed, Moses has not entered into the generic presence of God ("God is ambiguously everywhere") but rather he encounters the God of his ancestors who speaks directly to him and calls him by name. It is in the presence of the awesome mystery of God that he takes off his sandals—a gesture of humility. Keep in mind that the word *humility* is derived from Latin *humus*, which means of the earth, grounded, down to earth, of the soil. In this physical gesture, Moses recognizes that he is the creature, not the Creator. He is of the earth.

Given his recent history—fleeing into the wilderness after murdering an Egyptian slave master (Exod. 2:11–15a)—Moses might have thought that to be in the presence of the God of his ancestors was sufficient for the day, a remarkable occurrence in its own right. God calls him by name. God has not forgotten Moses: the Hebrew child, the Egyptian prince, and the defender of harassed women (Exod. 2:15b–22). But such was not the case. In this encounter on holy ground, Moses hears God speak: "I know the sufferings of my people, and I have come to deliver them from the Egyptians . . . I will send you to bring my people out of Egypt." (Exod. 3:1–5, 7–8, 10–12)

From shepherd to liberator in a few moments? Moses balks at the suggestion and then presents all the reasons why this directive will fail until that point where God's assurance of God's abiding presence with him diminishes his hesitation. From a life hidden in the wilderness, Moses becomes a public person with a mission that leads the Hebrew people from weary years of confinement, of enslaved oppression, and hopelessness into the open space of freedom and a common life guided by the covenant God makes with them at Mount Sinai—a covenant sealed with a shared meal.

For thousands of years, the Jewish people have celebrated this ancient act of liberation by gathering in homes for the Passover meal on a day aligned with the spring equinox in the northern hemisphere: the birth of life from winter's apparent death—the birth of a free community from the deathly world of slavery. The Passover meal includes food and drink that tells this story of redemption: eating parsley dipped in salt water represents the tears of oppression; eating bitter herbs marks the taste of a bitter life in slavery; the breaking and sharing of unleavened bread symbolizes the hasty departure in which there was no time for leaven to work; the drinking of four cups of wine during the meal signifies the four cups that express the four terms used by God for deliverance: "Say therefore to the Israelites, I am the LORD, and *I will free you* from the burdens of the Egyptians and *deliver you* from slavery to them. *I will redeem you* with an outstretched arm and with mighty acts of judgment. *I will take you as my people*, and I will be your God. You shall know that I am the LORD your God, who has freed you from the burdens of the Egyptians" (Exod. 6:6–7). The meal is interspersed with biblical readings that narrate this mighty act of deliverance, with questions about the meaning of the meal, and with psalms sung that give thanks to God.

And in many Jewish households, the ethical implications of keeping Passover are paramount: "Who does not enjoy freedom today? Who experiences various forms of bondage today? Whose life is marked by bitterness or despair today?" In asking such questions, another arises: "How might we respond to such suffering through action inspired by our keeping of this festival of freedom?" In other words, the ancient memory—enacted in a communal tradition of story and ritual—informs and guides a commitment to social justice in the present. We might say it this way: one eats and drinks the story of liberation so that it enters one's life and one's way of living in the world.

Story and Ritual

It should not surprise us that worship in the Jewish household was the matrix in which Christian worship emerged. After all, Jesus of Nazareth was a Galilean Jew of the first century who knew the biblical stories and practiced the communal rituals of his people. In reflecting on what they knew of his life, the authors of Mark, Matthew, and Luke agree that after his baptism in the Jordan River, he announced the good news of the coming reign of God, what Matthew calls the kingdom of heaven. Jesus spoke of this kingdom, this reign, with common images: seed falling on rocky ground and fertile soil (Mark 4:1–34); free healing for the poor (Matt. 4:23–25); unexpected generosity in wages (Matt. 20:1–16); a lowly mustard weed that grows rapidly (Luke 13:19); a woman kneading unholy leavened bread (Luke 13:20–21); a great dinner for the homeless (Luke 14:15–24). At first glance, his images may appear homely if not quaint, but when considered in their context, they become surprising: they prompt the listener to ask questions. In a world that viewed the homeless as literally nothing, as human waste, why give them free healing and thus prolong their misery? In the eyes of the world, a "kingdom" is something grand, a reality ruled over by a monarch: why would Jesus compare it to a fast-growing weed rather than a majestic cypress or sequoia? And how could something as unholy as leaven—yeast—serve as the sign of God's holy presence? Suddenly, the homely image begins to call into question conventional convictions and doesn't seem so quaint after all.

And yet Jesus not only spoke of the reign of God in human life, he also enacted it. He healed the sick on the Sabbath in violation of religious law (Luke 13:10–17); he was the object of criticism for eating and drinking with persons considered social outcasts, with persons who were not religiously observant (Mark 2:13–17); he touched the diseased and thus risked being associated with their illness and their exclusion from village life (Matt. 8:1–4); he offered mercy in an empire that viewed merciful acts as pathological behavior, as something "womanly" to be avoided by powerful men (Matt. 9:9–13); in a patriarchal culture, he welcomed women as equal to men, relied on their funding for his movement, and praised their intelligence (Luke 8:1–3); he healed those who because of race or ethnicity were viewed as unholy and to be avoided (Mark 7:24–30).

We should note his sayings and his actions were made *in public* for he spent the vast majority of his life in places other than centers of worship: by a lake, in a plain, or on a hilltop; at a market, in a home, or walking on a road. While Christians worship him in a church and Jews gather for the Sabbath liturgy in a synagogue, Jesus knew nothing of churches and was seen only rarely in a synagogue, at least according to the biblical narrative. In poetry and parable, he spoke good news to those who were thought to be socially inferior and far from God. His actions expressed the gospel of God's nearness among a people who were thought to be distant from God by virtue of their ethnicity, their work, their failure to observe religious practices, or their poverty. No wonder Matthew spoke of Jesus as Emmanuel, God with us, or Luke portrayed him as a liberator from religious or cultural stigma.

Symbol: There Is Always More

If the potent image and the public action were the primary means through which Jesus communicated the nearness of God's reign, God's presence in human life on earth, those startling images and unconventional practices were filled with more than one meaning. Perhaps this is why they are called *symbolic* words and actions: they overflow with significance; they cannot be reduced to one thing and thus easily controlled. Indeed, for those who prefer their religion neat and ordered, the sayings and actions of Jesus will be confounding because they resist containment and easy definition.

Consider for a moment the regular presence of bread in the ministry of Jesus. When given bread or taking it in his hands, he gives thanks, all the Evangelists tell us. But that giving thanks was offered to God for the fields that produced the barley and the human labor that harvested and ground the grain into flour. Bread is God's gift to sustain life on earth. Bread is a gift of the fields and human effort. And there is this, too: a loaf of bread was broken by hand into fragments so that it could be shared and then consumed. What we know of the meals of Jesus is that bread was shared equitably so that no one went hungry. Bread is nourishment and in the culture of Jesus, it was the staple food for the vast majority of the population—some 90 percent who lived in poverty. It was the bread of the poor. The poor lived with subsistence, not knowing if there would be sufficient food for the next day. Perhaps this is why Jesus's prayer includes this petition—"Give us this day our daily bread"—for the poor lived with constant anxiety: will there be bread for my hungry children? So bread is a gift of God for all people; a gift of the earth; the work of human labor; food to be shared rather than hoarded; the one thing needed to sustain life and stave off hunger; the staple provision of the poor. And there is this: that bread, which is for Christians the body of Christ, his very life *broken open and shared with the many* (see Matt. 25:26) rather than kept to himself. How can one word and one action—the sharing of bread—hold so many meanings? Rather than reducing meaning to one thing only, the language of biblical and sacramental faith moves one toward expansion, discerning more than what was first imagined.

The language of Christian worship, the language of faith, is not the prose of policy statements, talk show hosts, constitutions and bylaws, canons, or stand-up comedy, the language of the street, or the careful definitions of the academy. Rather, it is *primal language*: the discourse of story, parable, poetry, and visions. It is the language of metaphor that holds two things together in uneasy juxtaposition, always prodding the thoughtful Christian to ask how one can be related to another: how is it that the Messiah and Savior of the world is born in poverty rather than in a palace? What does it mean to call the pursuit of justice the foundation of God's throne? Why do the Gospels name Jesus a king only—only—as he reigns crucified from a tree? What, then, does it mean to worship a crucified God?

In a church or through digital means, we gather on a Sunday morning with these words: "Blessed be God: Father, Son, and Holy Spirit. And blessed be God's kingdom, now and forever. Amen." Throughout much of the year, we may then sing a canticle that acclaims the Holy Three as monarch, Lamb of God, Holy One, and Most High—each of the biblical images shedding peculiar light on the motive for our praise: the Holy Trinity, glorious in its remarkable diversity, overflows with mercy for this world, a mercy we rarely, if ever, experience in the kingdom of this world.

And that is the point: in the language of Christian worship, we enter into another vision of life than the one portrayed in the movies, seen on the computer screen, or viewed on television. That world, as entertaining and informative as it can be, does not set forth unconditional love and the pursuit of justice, the challenge to forgive rather than harm, and the difficult work of reconciliation as its primary values. That world, the one in which we live most of the time, frequently judges human worth based on the degree to which it can be economically productive, useful, or entertaining. That world does not speak of humans created in the image of God and endowed with an eternal dignity that asks for respect if not honor. While Christians live and serve in the kingdom of this world, their perception of this world is rightly guided by the vision set forth in the words and actions of Jesus Christ—those words and actions that are rehearsed from Sunday to Sunday in the holy Eucharist, and day by day in the Daily Office.

It is these ancient images and actions—this primal language—that are intended to rehearse the gathered assembly for life in public, for life in the world. Indeed it is not for nothing that the baptized and communed people of God—women, men, and children—are strangely called a holy priesthood, a term once reserved only for males from elite families. But the twist here is this: the priesthood shared among all the baptized, among this diverse group we call the church, is exercised in the world—in a world that yearns for a mercy and a justice it finds so difficult to generate.

We gather in homes and churches in the presence of the Mystery of God as revealed in Jesus Christ who is, for us, our Burning Bush: calling us into holy ground only then to send us forth.

Questions for Discussion

1. What is one biblical story that holds great significance for you? Why does it hold such significance in your life?

2. Is there a psalm text that you want sung at your funeral service? If so, what is the text and why would you want friends and family to remember you with this psalm?

3. Is there an action of Jesus or an event in his public life that holds meaning for you? What is it? Why is it important for you?

4. The psalms provide many images and metaphors of God. Is there one that you want to hear more in worship? If so, why?

2 ■ The Liturgy Orients Us to a Loving, Liberating, and Life-Giving Mission

> When he came to Nazareth, where he had been brought up, he went to the synagogue on the sabbath day, as was his custom. He stood up to read, and the scroll of the prophet Isaiah was given to him. He unrolled the scroll and found the place where it was written: "The Spirit of the LORD is upon me, because he has anointed me to bring good news to the poor. He has sent me to proclaim release to the captives and recovery of sight to the blind, to let the oppressed go free, to proclaim the year of the LORD's favor." And he rolled up the scroll, gave it back to the attendant, and sat down. The eyes of all in the synagogue were fixed on him. Then he began to say to them, "Today this scripture has been fulfilled in your hearing."
>
> (Luke 4:16–21)

This short passage from the Gospel of Luke presents what one might call the mission of Jesus, with the rest of the gospel flowing from that mission and giving indications of what such a mission looked like in first-century Palestine. Needless to say, the careful reader of the Gospel will recognize that the expression of that mission was no easy thing. Jesus met with criticism and opposition: from members of his family; from his disciples who frequently come across as blind to his purpose; from onlookers as well as religiously observant people who were disarmed if not bothered by his words and deeds; and, eventually, by the Roman authorities who put him to death in a cruel form of capital punishment.

For the past century and with more focused attention in the last fifty years, scholars of the New Testament have brought awareness to the *context* in which Jesus's public mission took place, that being the Roman Empire and Roman Palestine, an imperial colony. We hear hints of this in Luke's gospel when he mentions Emperor Augustus, Quirinius, governor of Syria, Pontius Pilate, and the Roman guard. Rather than serving simply as interesting "background" to the story of Jesus as portrayed in the Gospels, biblical scholars have pointed to the *tension* between the kingdom of God proclaimed by Jesus and the kingdom of Caesar that suffused the world in which Jesus and his followers lived. Their work invites Christians to reconsider why Jesus met with criticism and opposition and, eventually, with death. To be sure, no one was crucified in the ancient world because they were nice or kind. Is it possible that the public life of Jesus—one announced almost every Sunday among us in the gospel reading—called into question what many considered "normal" in their world then?

Consider for a moment the titles Jesus receives in the angelic announcement of his birth to shepherds, an announcement heard and sung by contemporary worshipping assemblies each Christmas Eve (Luke 2:11). Everyone in the ancient Mediterranean world knew *prior* to the birth of Jesus that only one person was known as Savior, LORD, Son of God, and Prince of Peace—and that was the Roman emperor, Caesar Augustus. By giving these titles to a Jewish infant born in poverty within a Roman colony, Luke is up to something. Is he not suggesting that in contrast to the violence, injustice, corruption, and stratified social world of the empire, the birth of Jesus heralds another way of living in the world, another way called the kingdom of God, a world in which God, not Caesar, rules and guides life? Only two chapters later we hear Jesus taking as his own mission the one portrayed by the prophet Isaiah: to bring good news to the poor, release to captives, recovery of sight to the blind, freedom for the oppressed, and a time of the LORD's favor. What did that mission look like in Luke?

In his public life, Jesus offers forgiveness and is accused of blasphemy (Luke 5:17–26). He shares food and drink with a despised tax collector—and thus shares his social status and ugly reputation—and is questioned over the propriety of his dinner companion (Luke 5:27–32). He defends his followers who pluck grain—engage in work—on the Sabbath, suggesting that meeting human need might be more important than keeping the law (Luke 6:1–5). In a culture and an empire that righted wrongs with brutal revenge, he counsels his followers to love their enemies and refuse to strike back at them (Luke 6:27–36). He liberates a man tormented by a troubling spirit, an action that provokes fear among the people (Luke 8:26–39). Not alone in his mission, he sends out his followers to announce "Peace" ("We carry no weapons to harm you") and bring healing to those in need (Luke 10:1–12). Through a vivid parable about a loose-living son, he reveals the compassionate heart of God for those who have made a mess of their lives as well as those who stand in judgment over them (Luke 15:11–32). He warns against self-indulgence and condemns greed, something that was blessed by cultural elites and political leaders (Luke 16:19–31). He defends poor widows evicted from their homes by religious leaders—women forced to pay a religious tax they cannot afford (Luke 20:45–47; 21:1–4). Is it any wonder that his mission—to promote the reign of God—would be met with opposition in an imperial culture that believed itself to be the greatest on the face of the earth, led by a man who styled himself as the savior of the world, a politician who used violent military force to expand his colonies and silence dissent?

And of course we know how the story ends: Jesus is betrayed, arrested, tortured, and executed in public—a warning to anyone who would promote another kingdom, another way of living in this world so at odds with what many took to be blessed by the pagan gods of the state. Perhaps as his body was taken down from the cross, the Roman guards concluded that his death would surely silence him and his movement. But such was not the case, as Paul was at pains to point out: Thus it is written, "The first man, Adam, became a living being; the last Adam [Christ] became a life-giving spirit" (1 Cor. 15:45). Against all conventional thought, the mission of Jesus did not die: it only expanded into the Mediterranean world and then throughout the globe.

Two Words Concerning Liturgy

Anglican/Episcopal spirituality has been marked by dialectical thinking for centuries. That is, we have valued holding two things (*dia*) together at the same time: poetry and scientific analysis, silence and speech, holy baptism and holy orders, faith and reason, movement and rest, tradition and change, education and experience, chant and jazz. The same can be said for Episcopal worship. We gather to worship the God who is revealed in the birth, life, death, and resurrection of Jesus Christ. We gather to give thanks—*eucharistia,* in the Greek—for the gift of salvation: God's offer of life, health, wholeness, healing, forgiveness, unconditional love, enlightenment, justice, and peace, to name only a few of the metaphors that expand the scriptural understanding of salvation. Though some forms of Christianity suggest that Christian worship is solely what Christians do *for* God, the witness of the New Testament suggests differently: it is God who first comes close to God's creation; it is God who advances in the person of Jesus Christ toward all that God has created, including the global human household. This is the mystery of the Incarnation: that God takes the initiative out of love to become one with God's creatures. For this we rightly give thanks whenever and wherever we gather for worship: in the home, a church, a park, or a summer camp.

As the sole purpose of worship, however, that view is limited. Consider the famous church musician, Johann Sebastian Bach, who signed all his sacred music compositions with these initials—SDG—*Soli Deo Gloria*: "to God alone be the glory." Bach expressed only one dimension of the Christian liturgy: giving glory or thanks to God. What was missing in this well-known Latin phrase was the second word, the ancient dismissal from the liturgy: *Ite, missa est*: "You all go, being sent forth." Or, as we pray after receiving communion: "Send us out to do the work you have given us to do" (Book of Common Prayer 366). This is to say that our common worship can never be reduced only to the worship of God, for the God we worship is revealed in the mission of Jesus and that mission takes place not primarily in church but in the world, in daily life. Or put another way: the advance of God toward this world continues *in* the world, in daily life, through the people of God. Christian liturgy is thus formation of the public body of Christ, the Christian community, in its worldly mission.

Indeed a focus only on the worship of God is likely to give the impression that singing the triune God's praise, hearing a consoling sermon, and receiving the Eucharist as if it were a private and personal moment between Jesus and me is more a clubby affair focused on the individual's need or community cohesion. Mention the words "evangelism" or "mission" to many Episcopalians and the response looks more like a cringe than an embrace. Perhaps that is so because Anglicans and American Episcopalians have enjoyed a privileged status for many decades if not centuries: the state church of England and the Commonwealth, with government subsidies; an American denomination with many well-educated members, endowed urban parishes, and a penchant for assuming that people will be attracted to this form of Christianity because of its beautiful music, charming vestments, and open-mindedness.

But worship that simply reinforces the status quo of a parish or diocese misses the second word of Christian liturgy: being sent forth to continue the mission of Jesus in daily life, what Michael Curry, the twenty-seventh presiding bishop of the Episcopal Church, calls *the loving, liberating, and life-giving mission of Jesus.* Said another way: the worship of the church is an ensemble of actions with words that are intended to form the gathered assembly for its apostolic life in the world. After all, a community that is *apostolic,* as being sent forth, will rightly see itself as baptized and communed for the sake of something else: "to proclaim by word and example the Good News of God in Christ, and to seek and serve Christ in all persons" ("The Baptismal Covenant," Book of Common Prayer 304–305). So the liturgy is an act of breathing in and breathing out, of gathering and sending, of celebrating the church's liturgy to continue the social liturgy, its mission, in daily life. To speak of the church's worship as apostolic is to reject the notion that the liturgy is simply a form of personal piety or an exercise in community cohesion to which any and every one is welcome.

A Challenge and a Promise

After he told his incredulous disciples for a third time that he would be arrested and put to death because of his public work, and after refusing yet again his disciples' request for privileged positions (Mark 10:32–37), Jesus asked them this potent question: "Are you able to drink the cup that I drink, or be baptized with the baptism that I am baptized with?" (Mark 10:38). Let us be clear: the cup was the cup of suffering and the baptism of which he spoke was his death on the cross. To affirm that his contemporary followers are called into a loving, liberating, and life-giving mission is not sweet rhetoric. Rather, it is the call to continue his mission in the world today—a mission that was met then with obstacles, criticism, mockery, skepticism, and intolerance. And yet it was a mission that actually brought good news to the poor, lifted up the lowly, illuminated the dignity of every human being, released people from debilitating forms of bondage, and shared food and drink across the invisible but powerful social borders of gender, race, and social status, creating a discipleship of equals and an equitable sharing of God's many earthy gifts.

Though the language of inclusion has recently swept through many parishes and dioceses and rightly invites Episcopalians to see the church as larger than its privileged past, the corollary to the first question—"Who is welcome?"—is the second question—"Welcomed into what?" You, whoever you are, are welcome to come and see this community of faith and find a home within it. But part of that welcome must include an orientation to the community's purpose, its mission in the world. One rightfully asks of anyone who will be washed into the life of the triune God and Christ's earthly Body: "Do you renounce the evil powers of this world which corrupt and destroy the creatures of God? Do you renounce all sinful desires that draw you from the love of God?" (Book of Common Prayer 302). Again, two words are needed, not just one: *welcome* but welcome for the sake of *mission* in daily life, in the world beyond the liturgy.

Though he was never asked the questions of the Baptismal Covenant, Dietrich Bonhoeffer, the German Lutheran martyr and beloved friend of many Episcopalians and Anglicans, knew well the reality of evil powers. What stunned this Lutheran pastor's conscience was the degree to which religiously observant German Christians who viewed their church as a consoling presence in life failed to question and resist the pernicious power of their legally elected government, the Nazis. What astonished Bonhoeffer was the failure of church leaders to ask the significant question: "Are you willing to participate in the mission of Jesus in public life?" It became apparent that few Christians in Germany were willing to drink the cup and be baptized with the baptism of resistance to the kingdom of their world. Indeed, that wicked kingdom promoted a distorted religion called "positive Christianity" in which no one would ever be asked to inconvenience him or herself by coming to the aid of their neighbor in need, in which the image of the suffering Christ—the crucifix—was removed from the churches and was replaced with the national flag. No, a loving, liberating, and life-giving mission—grounded in biblical story and sacramental practice—was not at the center of German worship. Bonhoeffer's church welcomed anyone who wanted to join. But its leaders and its people failed to ask what the mission of Jesus asked of them.

Surely, it can be different for us.

This is to say that when we begin to recognize the intrinsic relationship between communal worship and common mission, we can begin to hear and sing the biblical stories, parables, and sayings with ears attuned to their missional or worldly purpose. We can begin to recognize in worship the presence of the public Jesus who spent most of his life outside of worship even though he was a participant in the domestic and communal rituals of his people. We can begin to see that the rituals we enact are intended to draw us into the work of God in the world today. God does not need our worship; we need it.

To be sure, it is not easy to promote a loving, liberating, and life-giving mission in a nation and a world tragically divided by hate speech and political rancor; it's not easy to be liberated from racism and racial injustice or the prejudices to which we have been exposed by the dominant culture; nor is it easy to promote the health of this planet, God's earth, imperiled by pollution and climate change. And yet we are not alone—*we are not alone.* ". . . I am with you always, to the end of the age," promises the One no earthly power could silence (Matt. 28:20).

Questions for Discussion

1. Where do you see the mission of Jesus as portrayed in Luke 4 being enacted in your parish? Are there ways in which this mission can be strengthened?

2. How would a member of your town or city who is not religiously affiliated know that your parish is guided by a mission that takes place in daily life?

3. Early Christian historians note that people were attracted to the Christian faith because it demanded something of newcomers and called forth their commitment. Do you think such a commitment is heard today in the Episcopal Church? Should it not be heard? Yes? No?

4. Are there ways in which your parish helps parishioners who work in "secular" jobs recognize their work as a dimension of their Christian vocation in the world? Are there ways in which this connection can be strengthened?

3 ■ The Liturgy Asks
Life-Changing Questions

. . . Now there was an Ethiopian eunuch, a court official of the Candace, queen of the Ethiopians, in charge of her entire treasury. He had come to Jerusalem to worship and was returning home; seated in his chariot, he was reading the prophet Isaiah. Then the Spirit said to Philip, "Go over to this chariot and join it." So Philip ran up to it and heard him reading the prophet Isaiah. He asked, "Do you understand what you are reading?" He replied, "How can I, unless someone guides me?" And he invited Philip to get in and sit beside him . . . Then Philip began to speak, and starting with this scripture, he proclaimed to him the good news about Jesus. As they were going along the road, they came to some water; and the eunuch said, "Look, here is water! What is to prevent me from being baptized?" He commanded the chariot to stop, and both of them, Philip and the eunuch went down into the water, and Philip baptized him.

(Acts 8:27–31, 35–38)

The Acts of the Apostles is Luke's companion to and continuation of his Gospel. In both books, he was writing to Gentiles—non-Jews—who knew little of Judaism and Jesus' homeland. In this regard, Luke had the challenging task of communicating the significance of a Jewish Jesus to listeners with no experience of Palestine, the Hebrew scriptures, and Jewish ritual practice. Perhaps

Luke's task is little different than what contemporary Christians are called to do in nations that are increasingly secular, in which growing numbers of people have little experience of any religion: to effectively and persuasively communicate the significance of Christian faith and life to those who have experienced nothing of what long-time Christians take for granted.

What is surprising in Luke's story is that the main character is an unnamed Ethiopian eunuch who served as a royal treasurer. A eunuch was a male who had been painfully castrated in order for him to serve an elite woman, in this case a queen, with no chance of sexual relations. Males serving females in ancient patriarchal cultures stigmatized eunuchs as less than male; in a culture that prized male sexual prowess, castration rendered eunuchs infertile, sexually barren: half-men as it were. This is to say that the Ethiopian was a person of ambiguous sexual identity. The surprise of the story is that after his conversation with Philip, a deacon from Jerusalem, the eunuch asks if anything could prevent him from being baptized. Apparently, there was nothing: the two enter the water and Philip baptizes him. In the cultural world of Jesus, where gender and gender roles were strictly defined, where some would have been quick to exclude such ambiguity as well as an individual of another race, the act of baptism was the original and truly radical act of inclusion.

But something else is present in the story that should capture our attention: the eunuch, this seeker, asks for assistance in interpreting a passage of scripture. The deacon Philip becomes a catechist, a teacher, and demonstrates how the scriptures point to the

Good News present in Jesus of Nazareth. Luke notes that as their conversation continues, they come to a body of water where Philip baptizes this person marked by sexual ambiguity, a person of another race who has now become a disciple of Jesus Christ. Keep in mind the movement of the story: Philip is moved by the Spirit to serve as a companion to this man; there is a conversation in which Philip suggests that for Christians, Jesus Christ is the center of the scriptures; and, then, having contemplated the life of Jesus, there is baptism. It was this pattern of coming to the inclusive act of baptism that developed into the early Christian practice of baptismal formation. Why did such a process emerge?

Christians Are Made, Not Born

Luke was creating his two-volume work in the nineties CE, some sixty years after the life of Jesus. Not long after his writing was completed and circulated among early Christian communities, an imperial Roman governor in Roman Asia (modern-day Turkey) was interrogating Christians for their refusal to worship the image of the Roman emperor as if he were their god. The governor, named Pliny, notes that two women deacons, leaders in this early Christian community, report that they gather weekly before daybreak (Sunday was a work day) to sing the praise of Christ and share a meal. Pliny speaks of this "religious sect" as a "superstition" or "contaminant" that will "infect" the countryside unless it is stopped. Should they fail to renounce Christ and should they refuse to worship the emperor and the gods of the Roman state, they would be executed. Case closed.

What does this interrogation suggest? Christians were viewed with growing skepticism, if not intolerance. The state's threat of death could be used to coerce their rejection of Jesus Christ and the values and practices that flowed from his life into the communities that bore his name. By their manner of life, Christians acted differently than their Roman or Greek or Syrian neighbors. As Pliny pointed out with surprise, they actually took an oath *not* to commit the crimes of adultery, fraud, and theft. He was surprised by this?

Their common life was marked by what Romans considered a seditious worship in which Christ rather than the emperor was praised, and an "abnormal" and upsetting social ethic: viewing women and men as equals; rescuing newborns legally abandoned to the elements by fathers who wanted no more children; opposing the unhygienic practice of abortion that usually killed the mother; rejecting the widespread cultural institution of slavery; offering free, rudimentary nursing to anyone in need; providing shelter and food for widows and indigent women who had no family support; offering material assistance to other Christians in need. These were *not* the practices of the dominant culture but rather those that flowed from the public mission of Jesus. Indeed, such practices and Christian refusal to worship the gods of the state placed early Christians as outliers in the dominant culture.

And yet more and more people were attracted to this movement, what the Acts of the Apostles calls the Way (Acts 24:14). What, then, of Luke's story of an Ethiopian seeker becoming Christian through what we know as baptism? What became apparent among early Christians who lived in a culture that viewed them with considerable skepticism was the need to be clear on what it would mean to become Christian. This meant creating a process of formation for Christian faith and life, *a process of baptismal formation*: Philip's conversation with the Ethiopian was a microcosm of what Christians developed. Foremost in the minds of early Christian leaders was the mission of Jesus entrusted to his body, the local Christian community. Would someone shaped by the values and practices of the dominant imperial culture recognize the transformation needed to live and serve in a minority religious community? Rather than extend an open welcome to just anyone who was interested and draw them immediately into the table fellowship that marked the Sunday gathering, early Christians wanted to know if it was possible for an interested seeker to enter into ongoing conversion to the values and practices of the kingdom of God as revealed in Jesus Christ. Christians asked questions of those interested in joining the Christian community: Are you fully aware of what it means to become a Christian, to understand the scriptures, to pray with others, to reject the worship of the state, to find your life drawn into and guided by the life of Jesus Christ and this community of faith? Though early Christians clearly claimed that the LORD's Supper was the LORD's and not the church's property, their first question focused on discerning the capacity of a newcomer to participate actively in support of the community and its worldly mission. What we see here is an unwillingness to allow Christian values and practices to be assimilated into and thus compromised by those of the dominant culture.

Thus, we find a process developing in which those initially attracted were drawn gradually into Christian faith and life. For our ancestors in the faith, Christians were not born into a wholly Christian culture and into a church that would do nothing more than guide them through the predictable stages of life, from the cradle to the grave. Rather, they held that joining the community was its distinctive way of living in the world; a way of living that actually questioned and rejected many of the values and practices of the culture in which they lived. But they were also acutely aware of what the sociologist, Rodney Stark, calls the "free-rider" problem: people who were eager to receive the benefits of the Christian community but demonstrated little desire to accept the responsibilities of Christian life and to offer support to the community.[1]

Thus, the process of becoming Christian first asked inquirers why they were interested in joining this community: What is attractive to you? What questions do you have about our way of life? Were newcomers aware of the fact that Christians did not view commonplace revenge as a normal and moral way to respond to harm done to them? Did they recognize what alarmed Pliny: that women were leaders in a community that upheld the equality of all people created in the image of God and that people of ambiguous sexuality were welcomed? In light of a culture that thrived on dividing ethnicities and perpetuated an economic system fueled

---

1. Rodney Stark, *The Rise of Christianity: How the Obscure, Marginal Jesus Movement Became the Dominant Religious Force in the Western World in a Few Centuries.* San Francisco: HarperSanFrancisco, 1997.

by the labor of the poor and of slaves, did they know that baptism would introduce them to a community marked by diverse races and ethnicities, a community that strove to mitigate the inequalities of economic class: "There was not a needy person among them, for as many as owned lands or houses sold them and brought the proceeds of what was sold. They laid it at the apostles' feet, and it was distributed to each as any had need" (Acts 4:34–35)?

Such questions then led to a period in which those seeking baptism were introduced to the scriptures: one of the essential elements of Christian life and worship. How could they grasp what it meant to be Christian apart from the story of the Christian community, a story that Christians traced to the creation of the world, the emergence of the Hebrew people, and the life of Jesus, the Jewish prophet and Messiah of God? They were led to recognize that in contrast to the worship of the state and its incessant need to offer sacrifices to appease its capricious gods, Christians gathered to offer thanks to a loving and liberating God who asked that this loving and liberating power become manifest in their lives through service to their neighbors in need. In the first five centuries of Christian history, we find little evidence of the notion that newcomers should immediately grasp or understand what entailed Christian faith and Christian practice. What we *do* encounter are communities that served as centers of ongoing formation in Christian faith and life—a formative process that was shared by catechists (teachers), sponsors, deacons, musicians, bishops, lectors, treasurers, and artists—indeed, the entire parish.

It should be clear that an inquirer was free to leave this process at any time and reconsider their initial interest in becoming Christian. There were to be no forced marches into the kingdom of God as revealed in the life of Jesus and animated by his Spirit in succeeding generations. But if an inquirer found a home in the scriptures, the common prayer, and the worldly service of the Christian community, their preparation intensified in late winter as the church anticipated the celebration of Easter in the spring. This was the origin of Lent: a forty-day period of focused preparation by Christians to renew the vows of baptism and to celebrate the initiation of new members through baptism, anointing, and first communion at the Easter Vigil on Holy Saturday. Luke's narration of an encounter between a deacon of Jesus Christ and a man interested in understanding the scriptures—a conversation that led to baptism—had become a process of formation, preparing inquirers to enter the Christian community and share in its loving, liberating, and life-giving mission in the world.

Protection From the World or Service in It?

Early Christians experienced the liturgy as an ensemble of actions that revealed the living presence of the wounded and risen Jesus coming to them through baptism, through the Word of God proclaimed and interpreted in light of contemporary need, and most importantly, through the broken bread and shared cup of wine. As the church historian, Justo González rightly points out, early Christians celebrated the victory of Christ over evil and deathly powers and his presence in this world in the great sacraments of the gospel: baptism and Eucharist.

In time, however, this emphasis changed. By the early Middle Ages, increasing emphasis was on human sin as disobedience to the law of God; the remedy for this sin in sacramental absolution gained ground: not a cosmic victory by Christ over deathly and evil powers but rather the forgiveness of personal sin. By the eleventh century, much of Europe had become Christian: a veritable state religion in which clergy served as agents who registered births and baptisms, heard confessions of sin, registered and witnessed marriages, prayed with the sick, offered the last rites to the dying, and buried the dead: a ministry to the predictable stages of life in which pastoral focus shifted from preparing people to enter the mission of Jesus to preparing people for the afterlife. Today we witness this emphasis in the many collects of the prayer book that focus exclusively on the promise of eternal life. The urgent questions addressed to inquirers and the subsequent formation of adults and their families for Christian baptism were reduced to a few questions asked of parents at an infant's baptism: questions that focused on teaching the Ten Commandments, the creed, and the LORD's Prayer, with the promise to bring the child to church.

This emphasis in church life did not end with the reform movements of the sixteenth century. While Thomas Cranmer and his colleagues revised the church's worship in accord with a number of significant theological emphases, the imprint of a state religion and the church's service to the state—to create godly citizens of the monarch's realm—remained. Little did this emphasis change in the formation of the Episcopal Church in the United States. What was the primary purpose of baptism? To forgive one's sinful state entered at birth, to welcome one into "the congregation of Christ's flock," and to prepare the infant to "manfully fight under [Christ's] banner against the world and continue as Christ's faithful soldier unto his life's end" (The Book of Common Prayer 1789).

What surprised many Anglicans in Canada and Episcopalians in the United States was the recovery of the early Christian emphasis on holy baptism and the process of becoming Christian, an emphasis and process outlined in the American Book of Common Prayer 1979, various editions of the Book of Occasional Services, the Canadian Book of Alternative Services 1985, and the Anglican Rites for the Catechumenate 2019. Not only is the centrality of holy baptism as the source of Christian identity, ministry, and mission highlighted in the church's more recent liturgical practice, the question of joining the church's mission in the world has been made clearer in the questions asked of those coming to holy baptism: "Do you renounce the evil powers of this world which corrupt and destroy the creatures of God? Do you renounce all sinful desires that draw you from the love of God? Do you turn to Jesus Christ and accept him as your Savior? Will you proclaim by word and example the Good News of God in Christ? Will you seek and serve Christ in all persons, loving your neighbor as yourself? Will you strive for justice and peace among all people, and respect the dignity of every human being?" (Book of Common Prayer 302, 305).

Baptism is the action of the triune God in the life of an individual who is joined to the global community we call the body of

Christ, his visible and public presence in the world today. To be welcomed into this body is surely to be welcomed into the local parish. But there is more: To walk in newness of life is to walk into the mission of Jesus Christ. In contrast to medieval and reformation views of that mission—either as warfare against the world or protection from it—the restoration of mission as loving service in the world and the promotion of God's justice and peace therein is an integral dimension of Christian faith and life that flows from the font. For this we can say, "Thanks be to God," and given the challenge of such a mission, we should pray, "Come, Holy Spirit, come and fill the hearts of your people."

Questions for Discussion

1. How have you experienced the gift of baptism in your life?

2. In light of the early Christian process leading to baptism, how might baptismal formation be strengthened in your parish?

3. How might preaching and teaching, singing, and praying more clearly present the relationship between baptism and the loving, liberating, and life-giving mission of God in your parish?

4. The names of God are frequently phrases: YHWH, meaning I will be who I will be; Emmanuel, meaning God is with us; Jesus, the one who saves. How else might you think of naming or addressing God as the one who loves, liberates, and gives life?

4 ▪ The Liturgy Holds Tradition and Change Together

> Now on that same day two of them were going to a village called Emmaus, about seven miles from Jerusalem, and talking with each other about all these things that had happened. While they were talking and discussing, Jesus himself came near and went with them . . . Then beginning with Moses and all the prophets, he interpreted to them the things about himself in all the scriptures . . . When he was at the table with them, he took bread, blessed and broke it, and gave it to them. Then their eyes were opened, and they recognized him . . . That same hour they got up and returned to Jerusalem; and they found the eleven and their companions gathered together . . . Then they told what had happened on the road, and how he had been made known to them in the breaking of the bread.
>
> (Luke 24:13–15, 30–31, 33, 35)

When I ask newcomers to the parish where they think parish worship on Sunday comes from, they frequently respond with these answers: a printed program given to every worshipper; the priest; a parish committee; the Book of Common Prayer; "No idea" and "It just happens." We then invite someone to read aloud Luke 24:13–49, the gospel reading appointed for the Third Sunday of Easter in years A and B of the lectionary cycle.

Here we begin to see an interesting pattern emerging. Two followers of Jesus have left Jerusalem, in despair because of his

Crucifixion—what they think is the end of his movement. And then a stranger appears, walking beside them, asking why they are so downcast. They tell him of their hope in Jesus, their hope shattered by his death. ". . . he interpreted to them the things about himself in all the scriptures" (Luke 24:27). As the evening approaches, the two disciples invite him to join them for supper. He takes bread and in customary Jewish practice blesses God for the bread, breaks it apart with his hands, and then gives a fragment to each of them. In the gestures of taking, blessing, breaking, and giving, it dawns on them who the stranger is. At this point they have two options: They can stay put at a safe distance from the city or they can leave and walk farther away from Jerusalem, distancing themselves from what they might suspect are Roman guards searching out those who were associated with Jesus. Instead, they enter the city.

Encountering Christ Today

What we see in Luke's post-resurrection narrative are two disciples joined by a third person, a stranger. The number is significant in that Christian worship is not a private act but a communal one, marked by dialogue, by listening and responding, by giving thanks and eating together. I am mindful of the parishioner who once told me how disturbed she was by people entering the church and by a lively prelude played by the organist: "They intrude on my worship." Her comment expresses more of an American individualism ("My private time with God") than Christian communalism ("Where two or three are gathered in my name").

The two disciples then express their anguish: they come to this moment with the still hidden Christ unafraid to express their frustration. "One thing I greatly appreciate about the formality of Episcopal worship," said a newcomer at one of our baptismal formation gatherings, a woman who had left a nondenominational church, "is that there is little room for emotional manipulation by clergy and musicians—clergy telling you how you should feel and musicians forcing you to sing only happy lyrics. That was something I experienced in spades elsewhere. We were always being told that a genuine Christian is a *happy* Christian and that we should expect to have *fun* in worship. I remember the Sunday I returned to that church after a miscarriage and the depression that only deepened my sorrow and anger. 'Happy?' 'Fun?' That constant message drove me crazy. But here I discovered the Anglican love of the Psalms. You know: 'My God, why have you forsaken me?' That's exactly how I felt. Here, with this well-ordered liturgy, with the long silence that followed the singing of the Psalm, no one tried to 'fix' me or force me to be 'happy.' There was space and silence to express my grief. I felt as if my experience mattered and mattered to God. I'll take the truth of human experience any day over emotional hijacking."

Next to the sadness of two disheartened disciples, Jesus places the scriptures. But note that he doesn't just place the scriptures before them and say, "Figure it out on your own." Rather, he interprets what was for them an ancient text in light of their contemporary need. He interprets the ancient texts—Moses, the covenant, and the prophetic call to reform—as images of who he

41

is and what he does. While the Bible can be read as interesting ancient literature, as its own kind of history, or as a book of rules, the current list of biblical readings selected for proclamation, interpretation, song, and prayer focus on Christ, on Christ who speaks in the present to the needs, frustrations, and hopes of those gathered around the Word of God. No wonder that worshipping assemblies stand and acclaim the reading of the gospel, frequently accompanied with torches and burning incense, making the sign of the cross and bowing.

While it can be tempting to imagine that the biblical readings appointed for each Sunday in the church's lectionary transport worshippers back to the first century in Palestine, the liturgy is not a journey to Bibleland in which sermon and hymns imagine what it was like to be with Jesus. Rather, the ancient texts through which the Spirit speaks are for us in the twenty-first century. They "read" our situation in life and, with a gifted preacher and lyricist, speak to our woe and our hope. Not long ago, I was horrified to hear a priest announce at a clergy conference that she simply tells jokes on Christmas and Easter when so many visitors are in church: "That's what they're looking for, right? A good time, a good laugh!" One has to wonder, then, about the woman sitting in the pew who just experienced a miscarriage or the man who lost his job: how is the Spirit speaking to them through the biblical readings, speaking the truth of their situation and the greater truth of God's presence with them in the here and now? Jokes? I don't think so.

In the ancient Mediterranean, an invitation to supper was not unusual: These were cultures that considered hospitality to strangers a primary responsibility. Indeed, the sharing of food and drink with guests presumed a social bond among the participants. At table, then, the two watch as their companion takes bread, blesses, breaks it, and gives it to them. In this regard, he followed ordinary Jewish table practice as he blessed God in these or similar words: "Blessed are you, LORD our God, Ruler of the universe, you who have brought bread forth from the earth." For a loaf of bread to be shared, then, it must be broken so that the many might eat from the one bread. It is in this moment and with this action that "their eyes were opened, and they recognized him." Luke notes that their hearts had glowed as the risen Christ interpreted the scriptures but, he continues, they recognized him—*recognized him*—in the ordinary action of taking, blessing, breaking, and offering bread to his table companions.

Keep in mind that after this encounter the two disciples, no longer disheartened, could stay in Emmaus. They could distance themselves from Jerusalem. Instead, they get up and go to the city. They enter that place of betrayal and loss with the news of the Resurrection. Their initial sadness, their disappointed hope, is transformed by this encounter with Christ in the scriptures and at the eucharistic table—a transformation that empowers them to enter the world with surprisingly good news.

Invitations and Instructions

We might imagine that Luke is simply describing a significant event of the past that took place on the Sunday after Jesus's death. Yet that was not his primary purpose. He was writing to Gentile

"God lovers" toward the end of the first century, people who asked an understandable question: "Where will we encounter the wounded and risen Christ today?" His answer is the story: in the *gathering of your assembly* wherever it may be; in the *hearing and interpretation of scripture* for your current need; in the taking, blessing, breaking, and *eating of bread with drinking from a wine cup*; in your *being sent into the world*, guided by the actions and words of this gathering. Luke is saying this: he comes to you through the assembly, the Scriptures, and the breaking of the bread, so that you might be witnesses to his wounded and risen life in the world—not just wounded and not just risen, but both held together—held together for the woman wounded in her soul by a miscarriage, for the man who lost his job and the two of them yearning for the resurrection of their lives.

The earliest description of Christian worship was written by a Christian convert named Justin Martyr in the middle of the second century: "On the day called Sunday, all who live in cities or in the country gather together to one place. Then the records of the apostles or the writings of the prophets are read for as long as time allows. When the reader has finished, the president instructs and encourages us to imitate these good things. Then we all stand together and offer prayers. When our prayer is finished, bread and wine and water are brought [to the table], and the president offers thanksgiving to the best of his ability, and the people give their assent [to the thanksgiving], saying Amen. Then there is a distribution and everyone participates in the bread and wine over which thanks have been given. These gifts are sent with the deacons to those who are absent. Those who are well off, and willing, give what they desire; and what is collected is deposited with the president who sees to the care for orphans and widows, those who, through sickness or any other cause, are in want, those who are imprisoned, and the workers sojourning among us. In a word, he looks after all who are in need."

Justin's description bears a striking resemblance to the pattern we see in Luke 24. But there is more: there is a reader, a president who presides at the gathering, deacons who bring the consecrated bread and wine to those who cannot join the gathering, the well-off individuals who contribute to a common fund, and a large group of people who receive material assistance from those who have gathered. After the presider's interpretation of the writings, all stand for the prayers. Bread, wine, and water are brought to the table; a bit of water is poured into the cup so that the young can drink the wine. The people give their verbal assent to the thanksgiving over bread and wine. And then, at the end of the liturgy, funds are collected to meet the material needs of the many, from orphans to sojourning workers. That is, the generosity of God received in the eucharistic gifts of bread and wine is extended and expanded toward those in need. Indeed, such generosity constitutes a significant dimension of the Christian mission in the world. This collection resembled Paul's work to gather a collection for suffering Christians in first-century Jerusalem (see 1 Cor. 16:1–4). Indeed, the collection described by Justin is one of the first instances of social assistance mentioned outside the New Testament.

Within a few centuries, the liturgical pattern we witness in Justin, a pattern bearing remarkable resemblance to the one we have discerned in Luke, will be elaborated differently among eastern Christians—in the Liturgy of St. John Chrysostom—and among western Christians—in the Mass of the Roman Rite—and with variations from northern France to southern Ethiopia, from Spain to western China. And yet the pattern itself was not lost. It was followed by medieval Christians in the British Isles in what historians call the Sarum Rite, the form of worship originating in the Diocese of Salisbury during the eleventh century. The pattern was sustained by Thomas Cranmer in the creation of the first Book of Common Prayer in 1549 and thus became the structure of eucharistic worship in the first American Book of Common Prayer of 1789. The same pattern is present in The Book of Common Prayer 1979 in its description of an order for celebrating the holy Eucharist: The people and the priest gather in the LORD's Name; Proclaim and Respond to the Word of God *with readings from scripture and always a reading from the Gospel*; Pray for the World and the Church; Exchange the Peace; Prepare the Table; Make Eucharist *using the Great Thanksgiving with the assembly's responses*; Break the Bread; and Share the Gifts of God (400–401).

One might conclude that the origin of the worship we hold today comes from the Bible. I am mindful of the young college student, raised in a conservative evangelical church, who once asked me with a troubled tone, "Why don't you have Bibles in your church pews?" In a gentle conversation of considerable length, we discussed the number of biblical readings proclaimed and sung in the liturgy—far more, he acknowledged, than the two verses selected by the preacher of his church for a lengthy Bible study during worship. We discussed the fact that the lectionaries for daily Eucharist and the Daily Office appoint biblical readings that would lead one through much of the Bible in a year. And we considered the enormous amount of scripture presented as liturgical text in the prayer book. The student's conclusion after our discussion? "So, you actually have a Bible service here." In many respects, he was correct.

And yet the New Testament is a reflection of the worship that existed among early Christians *prior* to the writing of gospels and letters and prior to the consensus that produced a list of books constituting the New Testament. Paul and Mark, Matthew and Luke, and John wrote for already-worshipping Christian communities. What is the origin of this pattern of worship that continues to awaken Christians to faith in God and love for their neighbors? Why, it is a living gift from earlier generations of Christian communities: a pattern rooted in the worship of the earliest Christ followers and their adaptation of Jewish ritual patterns to announce the gospel of Jesus Christ. To say the least, it is a resilient pattern that has proved adaptable in a variety of cultural settings. Why is that so?

When asked the very reasonable question of how God communicates with the human household, the ancient response has been as follows. In ways in which humans can receive that communication: through all the senses, and most especially through actions and words. For Christians, that communication is not generic. We hold that God yearns to communicate with the creation, little differently than loving parents yearn to be in relationship with their children. How do we come to know each other? Through words and actions, gestures and movement. "We declare to you what was from the beginning, what we have heard, what we have seen with our eyes, what we have looked at and touched with our hands, concerning the word of life—this life was revealed, and we have seen it and testify to it, and declare to you the eternal life that was with the Father and was revealed to us" (1 John 1:1–2).

Luke and Justin and the Sarum Rite and the Book of Common Prayer and the liturgy celebrated among us bear witness to the pattern of a people gathering in assembly for the proclamation of the Word of God and its interpretation, for the prayers in which the needs and suffering of the world enter into our collective consciousness, for the washing in water with anointing we call baptism, for thanksgiving at the eucharistic table with eating and drinking the presence of Christ, and for sending into the world. All these primary actions invite the assembly to give thanks for "the grace of our LORD Jesus Christ, the love of God, and the communion of the Holy Spirit" (2 Cor. 13:14). But there is more: these central things lead us into the mission of the wounded and risen Christ in the world. *Soli Deo Gloria*—to God alone be glory—and *Ite, Missa Est*—You all go, being sent—belong to each other, not one without the other.

Questions for Discussion

1. Do you prepare for Sunday's liturgy by reading the appointed biblical texts ahead of time? If this is a new practice, why not give it a chance for a month and see what it stirs up in you?

2. Rather than an imaginative return to the first century, the sermon is intended to be an interpretation of the biblical readings, one that responds to the needs and situation of the assembly and the world today. Do you regularly hear how the biblical texts shed light on life today? Or do you hear something else?

3. Portions of the great thanksgiving or eucharistic prayer are said or sung by the presider. But other portions of the thanksgiving are sung and spoken by the assembly. Do you sense your active participation in this culminating act of the Holy Communion? If not, why not?

4. This communal prayer is made after all have received communion: "Eternal God . . . you have fed us with spiritual food in the Sacrament of [Christ's] Body and Blood. Send us now into the world in peace . . . to love and serve you" (Book of Common Prayer 365). What is one way in which you or your parish extends the sacrament into the world?

5 ▪ The Liturgy Leads Us to the Seasons of Life on God's Earth

We who live in North America know well twenty-four-hour days, twelve-month years, paydays, sales days, tax days, quarterly reviews, and annual reports—a way of marking time in largely economic terms. Not surprisingly, time is experienced by many people in terms of cost: a wage per hour; billing clients in ten-minute increments; time as an "investment" in a project; buying someone's time; overtime pay. "Time is money." "That's not worth my time." With federal holidays and vacation days, much of our sense of time is shaped by secular values and timekeepers. And with the advance of artificial light, work can go on perpetually—24/7/365—matched by a constant stream of cable news and active social media sites. It would seem that many others are actually keeping time for us, whether we know it or not. What, then, of the Christian marking of time, of days, weeks, and seasons?

A Day Filled with Promise

For two thousand years, Christians have worshipped on Sunday, the first day of the week in the ancient Jewish calendar, the day following Saturday's rest. "But on the first day of the week, at early dawn, they came to the tomb, taking the spices that they had prepared. They found the stone rolled away from the tomb, but when they went in, they did not find the body" (Luke 24:1–3). "On the day called Sunday," wrote Justin Martyr, "all who live in cities or in the country gather together to one place" (*1 Apology* 67). The juxtaposition of the resurrection of Jesus with an ordinary workday should not be lost on us. He was not raised from death on a religious feast day or national holiday at high noon but rather in the darkness that preceded the dawn, on a day when people were just beginning to rise from sleep. Should we find him only in high holy days? No, the risen Christ is present in ordinary, common, workday time—the time in which we live most of our lives.

The morning of the third day, the day of the Resurrection, was marked by the light of the rising sun. The juxtaposition of his resurrection with dawning light should also gain our attention. It should not surprise us that celestial symbolism would become a primary way in which the Bible speaks of Christ: ". . . Where is the child who has been born king of the Jews? For we observed his *star* at its rising . . ." (Matt. 2:2). "When Jesus had been baptized . . . suddenly *the heavens* were opened . . . and a voice from heaven said, 'This is my Son, the Beloved, with whom I am well pleased'" (Matt. 3:16–17). ". . . Jesus took with him Peter and James and his brother John and led them up a high mountain, by themselves. And he was transfigured before them, and his face shone like *the sun*, and his clothes became dazzling white" (Matt. 17:1–2). "From noon on, *darkness* came over the whole land until three in the afternoon. And about three o'clock Jesus cried with a loud voice, 'Eli, Eli, lema sabachthani?' that is, 'My God, my God, why have you forsaken me?'" (Matt. 27:45–46). ". . . an angel of the LORD, descending from heaven, came and rolled back the stone and sat on it. His appearance was like *lightning*, and his clothing white as snow" (Matt. 28:2–3). From his birth to his resurrection, the sun, the stars, and the heavens witness to Jesus Christ as God's light and God's gift for the world. What did John record him saying? "I am *the light* of the world" (John 8:12).

But consider this: without the sun, there is no life on earth. We are a sun-dependent creation that includes humans and extends to many other creatures, to flora, fauna, and fish. In this regard, we might say that almost all creatures are equal in needing light to grow, gather nourishment, maintain health, engage in labor, and have a sense of time and its movement: from dawn to mid-day, from evening to night. "God said, 'Let there be lights in the dome of the sky to separate the day from the night; and let them be for signs and for seasons and for days and years, and let them be lights in the dome of the sky to give light upon the earth'" (Gen. 1:14–15).

For Jews and Christians, the sun and its light is more than an astronomical fact; it is a gift of God, its apparent "rising" and "setting" is the first way that humans gain a sense of time. While we may yearn for the warmth and the light of the sun, the sun itself is a creature of the triune God. Thus, the psalmist offers this invitation: "Praise the LORD, sun and moon; sing praise, all you shining stars. Praise the LORD, heaven of heavens, and you waters above the heavens. Let them praise the name of the LORD who commanded and they were created" (Ps. 148:3–4).

For two thousand years, Christians have worshipped as the sun rises on a Sunday morning to give thanks to God for the gift of life and the gift of salvation revealed in Jesus Christ. They have gathered, and we with them, on this day, the sun's day, to praise the One who is the ultimate source of all life, who enlightens ignorance, brings life out of apparent death, and offers new beginnings where we might experience endings and seemingly closed doors. No wonder our ancestors in the faith greeted Sunday as the day marked by hope: hope for themselves, hope for earth's people, and hope for the earth itself.

Yet the Christian liturgy is not only about thanksgiving and praise; it is also about supplication. We see this fundamental pattern of thanksgiving yielding to supplication in the collects and the thanksgiving prayers over the waters of baptism, the scented oil we call chrism, and the bread and wine of the Eucharist: "O God, whose blessed Son made himself known to his disciples in the breaking of the bread: open the eyes of our faith that we may behold him in all his redeeming work" (Collect, Wednesday in Easter Week, Book of Common Prayer 223); "We thank you for the gift of water. Over it the Holy Spirit moved in the beginning of creation . . . Now sanctify this water by the power of your Spirit" ("Thanksgiving over the Water," Book of Common Prayer 306–307).

Christians give thanks for what God has done in the distant and immediate past (as if God needed to be reminded of what God has done!) and then—and then—ask God to continue such action in the present—in, with, and through the people of God: "In the same way, let your light shine before others, so that they may see your good works and give glory to your Father in heaven" (Matt. 5:16); "But you are a chosen race, a royal priesthood, a holy nation, God's own people, in order that you may proclaim the mighty acts of him who called you out of darkness into his marvelous light" (1 Pet. 2:9).

To worship, then, on Sunday is to become truly conscious of the gift of God's light in the heavens—the sun, moon, and stars—and the greater gift of Christ the light whose presence nurtures and guides Christian faith and life. To worship on Sunday is to be renewed as witnesses to the Light. To worship on Sunday is to give thanks, a thanksgiving that yields to supplication for other people, their communities, and the earth. To worship on the LORD's Day is, in one real sense, to be free of the economy that too easily manipulates our priorities, free of the media that shapes and often distorts our desires, free of the demand to measure human worth only by one's productivity and usefulness. To enter into the worship of the LORD Day's, Sunday, is to receive through the liturgy a different vision of how life together might be lived: for here in the liturgy, the mission of Jesus can become clear in the preaching, singing, praying, and equitable sharing of God's gifts.

A Week With an Earth-Loving God

Yet Sunday is not the only day on which Christians worship. The first creation story presents seven days—the week—not only as a measure of time but more importantly as God's gift to the human household (Gen. 1:1–2:3). It was the week itself that became the opportunity for individual and communal prayer: "Seven times a day I praise you for your righteous ordinances" (Ps. 119:164). These seven times became the schedule for daily prayer in early Christian monastic communities. Given the monastic evangelization of the

British Isles that began in the sixth century, it should not surprise us that the Divine Office—praying each day of the week—became a part of English Christian spirituality. That is, as they established monasteries and parishes, the monks of St. Benedict introduced the divine office as a *parish practice* for those who entered the Christian faith through baptism. This practice was simple in its elements: the singing and recitation of psalms, scripture reading, and prayer for the church and world. Thus a love of the divine office was planted in English spiritual soil, perhaps kept occasionally in rural parishes but celebrated regularly and fully in cathedrals throughout the land.

A thousand years later, it was the genius of Thomas Cranmer to maintain the marking of each day with "Matyns" (morning prayer) and "Evensong" (evening prayer) in his creation of the Book of Common Prayer. For generations of Anglicans and Episcopalians, the service of Morning Prayer with sermon served as the primary form of Sunday worship until the nineteenth century recovery of the Eucharist as the primary order for Sundays, a recovery that has profoundly shaped liturgical spirituality and theology for Episcopalians and other member denominations of the Anglican Communion.

While Cranmer appointed two forms of daily prayer in the 1549 Book of Common Prayer, the American prayer book of 1979 also includes "An Order of Service for Noonday" and "An Order for Compline" (night prayer before retiring). Taken together, the four daily prayer services lead the household and the parish from the rising of the sun, to its apogee in the sky, and from its gradual setting in late afternoon and evening, to the utter darkness of night when stars and moon can be seen with greater clarity. Keep in mind that the practice of daily prayer has never been structured by an artificial schedule but rather tied to the movement of the sun and to celestial symbolism. Consider, for instance, the biblical sentences that begin Morning Prayer II in the Book of Common Prayer 1979: "Watch, for you know not when the master of the house will come, in the evening, or at midnight, or at cockcrow, or in the morning; lest he come suddenly and find you asleep" (Mark 13:35–36); "Nations shall come to your light, and kings to the brightness of your dawn" (Isaiah 60:3); "From the rising of the sun to its setting my Name is great among the nations . . ." (Malachi 1:11); "O send out your light and your truth; let them lead me; let them bring me to your holy hill and to your dwelling" (Ps. 43:3). Compline or Night Prayer presents a similar pattern: "You shall not be afraid of any terror by night, nor of the arrow that flies by day" (Ps. 91:5); "Come, bless the LORD, all you servants of the LORD, who stand by night in the house of the LORD" (Ps. 134:1); "Be our light in the darkness, O LORD" (Collect for Compline, Book of Common Prayer 133).

For modern urban dwellers whose sense of time is largely dictated by a work schedule that can now run for 24 hours, 7 days a week, the practice of daily prayer—even one form of daily prayer—can orient one to the larger rhythms of earth and skies. That the sun—not a desk lamp—gives life to all creatures merits not only our attention but also our praise. Thus, the power of the psalms is their unusual ability to call upon all creation to give God thanks: "The heavens are telling the glory of God . . . Day to day pours forth speech, and night to night declares knowledge" (Ps. 19:1–2); "Let the heavens be glad, and let the earth rejoice . . . let the field exult, and everything in it. Then shall all the trees of the forest sing for joy " (Ps. 96:11–12); "Let the floods clap their hands; let the hills sing together for joy at the presence of the LORD . . ." (Ps. 98:8–9).

Night declares knowledge? Earth rejoices, fields exult, and trees sing for joy? Floods have hands that clap? What is the modern Christian to make of these anthropomorphisms? Are they nothing more than pre-scientific hyperbole? Yet before we walk past these earthy metaphors, it might be good to remember that the God we worship on Sunday and in the Daily Office is the One who loves the entire creation—a good creation and a tangible reflection of the triune God's creative power and love of diversity. Or say it this way: at its best, Anglican spirituality is *ecophilic*; it loves all that God freely gives in and through creation. The singing or praying of the psalms thus possesses the power to shape an earth-loving spirituality, one that sees human beings within the earth and its many creatures rather than above the earth, dominating and using the earth and its creatures purely for human ends. Perhaps this is why the practice of praying or singing the psalms counters the tendency alive among some Christians to think that earth and the bodies of the earth—bodies of water, human bodies, animal bodies—are of little value, the intangible human soul, the one and only thing worthy of attention. No, the psalms say. No, the liturgy says: matter—tangible, touchable, earthy matter—truly *matters* for it is a living gift of the Creator and the means through which the intangible presence of God becomes one with human life.

A Year with the Cosmic Christ

It should not be difficult to recognize why the liturgical year is intimately wed to the changing seasons of the earth. It's not for nothing that within a largely agricultural economy the four seasons of the year, from spring to winter, became witnesses to Christian festivals marking the advent, birth, public ministry, death, and resurrection of Jesus, and the growth of the Christian movement. The lambing season at the vernal equinox; the wheat harvest in late spring; the greatest measure of daylight at summer's solstice; the grape harvest in late summer; the chilling of air and land in autumn; the greatest measure of darkness at winter's solstice—all these were turned, in the Christian imagination, toward marking the presence of the earth-loving Word of God through whom "all things came into being" and in whom "was life, and the life was the light of all people" (John 1:3–4). Consider, for instance, the ways in which Christians welcome the gifts of the earth into their homes and churches throughout the seasons of the year: the evergreen wreath of Advent; the Christmas tree, the Tree of Life; budding amaryllis and paper whites, Christmas cactus, and poinsettia; the blessing of local waters at Epiphany; the marking of ash from burned palms on the forehead; blessed palms or pussy willows adorning sacred images; a wood cross for veneration on Good Friday; the towering beeswax candle of the Easter Vigil; the flowing water of the font; scented olive oil—chrism—glistening on the forehead of the newly baptized; pungent incense; forsythia, tulips, hydrangea, lilies, and snapdragons; colored eggs; Rogation Day blessing of gardens, orchards, and fields; Pentecost bonfires and a showering of rose petals on the dining table as floral tongues of fire; herbs and flowers gathered around an image of Mary in mid-August; and the All Souls blessing of graves with lights, evergreens, herbs, and flowers.

For two thousand years amid the distinctive cultures of the world, Christians have drawn on the rhythms of earth's seasons and welcomed nature's gifts to praise the God revealed in Jesus Christ who is life for the world, for this earth and its many creatures. In this regard, the Bible and the liturgy present the cosmic Christ: "He is the image of the invisible God, the firstborn of all creation; for in him all things in heaven and on earth were created, things visible and invisible . . . in him all things hold together" (Col. 1:15–17). As the sixteenth-century reformer, Martin Luther, taught: in the resurrection, Christ was not seated on a throne in the distant heavens but rather raised into the presence and power of God throughout the cosmos. He has truly become a life-giving presence. Thus, he pervades all things, said Luther—the smallest leaf, the tiniest grain—yet cannot be contained and controlled therein. While western Christians have often focused on the birth, life, and death of Jesus—consider the ubiquity of the empty cross or crucifix in churches and homes— attention to the cosmic Christ who "gather up all things in himself, things in heaven and things on earth" (Eph. 1:10) asks for our attention—especially in this time of global warming and continued pollution of God's earth.

That Christians welcome the gifts of the natural world into their churches and homes is not simply a quaint reminder of Christianity's agricultural origins. Rather, it is the call to every Christian and every Christian community to ask, "What does this mean?" If we sing, read, and pray with celestial and terrestrial symbolism on Sunday, during the week, and throughout the seasons of the year, and if earth's many gifts play such a significant role in the Bible, liturgy, and an ecophilic spirituality, what is asked of us? The Canadian Book of Alternative Services concludes the promises of the Baptismal Covenant with this question: "Will you strive to safeguard the integrity of God's creation, and respect, sustain and renew the life of the Earth?" (Book of Alternative Services 159). In this time of earth's decline due to human actions that have emerged over the past 200 years beginning with the Industrial Revolution, this baptismal promise can shape the affections and actions of baptized people of God; it merits not only our attention but more importantly our study and concerted advocacy. For this, too, is now an integral dimension of the mission of Jesus, the mission of the cosmic Christ and his body alive in the world—a Body that rightly exists not for itself, but for nothing less than the life of the world.

Questions for Discussion

1. What challenges do you encounter in keeping Sunday as the LORD's Day—a day for gathering in assembly around the word, the font, and the eucharistic table?

2. Does your parish celebrate the Divine Office or one of its form (for example, Morning Prayer or Evening Prayer)? If not, how might you encourage this deeply Anglican practice? And what about practicing one brief form of daily prayer for a season of the church year? You will find brief services for use in the home in the Book of Common Prayer, 136–140.

3. What is your favorite season of the liturgical year? What about it makes a time to look forward to every year?

4. How is care for God's creation made known and guided in your life and your parish?

Lexicon

Altar: from Latin, *altare*, podium; a stone or wood table where gifts—grain, wine, or animal—were, in Israel's history, shared with God and the people of God

Assembly: the people gathered for worship with their leaders

Baptism: from Greek, *baptizo*, to dip; in Christian use, water washing in the Name of God accompanied by anointing with prayer, clothing in an alb, receiving a burning candle, and first communion

Catechumenate: from Greek *catechein*, the ability to hear well; the ancient and contemporary process of initial preparation of newcomers for Christian faith and life, leading to holy baptism and holy Eucharist

Chrism: from Greek *christos*, anointed one, as in Jesus Christ or Jesus the Messiah; olive oil mixed with fragrance; used in baptismal anointing, marking the newly baptized as a *christos*

Creation: biblical term for the natural world and all that inhabits the earth in the waters, on the land, in the skies; the triune God's continuously flowing gift

Daily Office: from Latin *officium*, responsibility or duty; sometimes referred to as the Divine Office or Liturgy of the Hours; communal or individual prayer at set times throughout the day and night with Psalms, scripture reading, and prayer

Ecumenism: from Greek *oikumene*, household; the efforts of separated Christians to grow in and toward greater unity in worship, learning, and service in the world

Eucharist: from Greek *eucharistia*, thanksgiving; specifically in reference to the eucharistic liturgy beginning with the presentation of bread, wine, and water, and concluding with the dismissal; generally, as in holy Eucharist, a reference to the entire service of the Word and sacrament

Font: from Latin *fons*, source; originally a flowing river or creek, a pool of water, and then a basin of water in which an adult or child was washed in the Name of God

Inclusive and expansive language: language used in worship that recognizes the great diversity of the assembly (for example, the movement from "men" to "sisters and brothers" to "siblings" or "friends of God") as well as the effort to expand the many metaphors of the Bible to describe God who is beyond gender and race

Lectionary: from Latin *lectio*, reading; the list of biblical readings appointed for worship, as well as the book in which the readings are printed for proclamation in the liturgy

Liturgy: from Greek *leitourgia*, work of the people; in Christian use, the actions and words of the assembly under the guidance of the Holy Spirit

Metaphor: the linking of two apparent contradictions to provoke a question ("How is this related to that?") and thus reveal a new insight

Mission: from Latin *missio*, being sent; the purpose of the Christian and the Christian community

Presider: the one who leads or guides worship, lay or ordained

Psalter: the book of Psalms in the Bible and in the Book of Common Prayer

Sacrament: from Latin *sacramentum*, originally an oath between leader and followers to remain with each other through good and bad times; in Christian use, an ordinary thing or action through which God communicates God's presence

Sacramentality: in Christian use, the recognition that created realities including human experience can potentially reveal the presence of God

Symbol: from Greek *symbolein*, to throw things together; a person, object, word, action, or artifact that possesses more than one meaning

Table: in Christian use, where early Christians gathered for readings from the Bible and for giving thanks over bread and wine for creation, redemption, and the presence of the risen Christ, with eating and drinking

Triune God: the Christian conviction that God is not a monad but rather a community of persons marked by diversity at the heart of all life

Select Bibliography

Brown, Raymond E. *Christ in the Gospels of the Liturgical Year.* Ronald Witherup, ed. Collegeville, MN: The Liturgical Press, 2008.

Curry, Michael B. *Following the Way of Jesus*, Vol. 6 in the *Church's Teachings for a Changing World.* New York: Church Publishing, Inc., 2017.

Davidson, Dent, and Lee, Jeffrey. *Gathered for God*, Vol. 8 in the *Church's Teachings for a Changing World.* New York: Church Publishing, Inc., 2018.

Galli, Mark. *Beyond Smells & Bells: The Wonder and Power of Christian Liturgy.* Brewster, MA: Paraclete Press, 2008.

Herbert, A.G. *Liturgy and Society: The Function of the Church in the Modern World.* London: Faber & Faber, 1942.

Meyers, Ruth A. *Missional Worship, Worshipful Mission: Gathering as God's People, Going Out in God's Name.* Grand Rapids, MI: Wm. B. Eerdmans Publishing, 2014.

Ramshaw, Gail. *Liturgical Language: Keeping It Metaphoric, Making It Inclusive.* Collegeville, MN: The Liturgical Press, 1996.

Stark, Rodney. *The Rise of Christianity: How the Obscure, Marginal Jesus Movement Became the Dominant Religious Force in the Western World in a Few Centuries.* San Francisco, CA: HarperSanFrancisco, 1997.

Torvend, Samuel. *Still Hungry at the Feast: Eucharistic Justice in the Midst of Affliction.* Collegeville, MN: The Liturgical Press, 2019.

Torvend, Samuel. *Flowing Water, Uncommon Birth: Christian Baptism in a Post-Christian Culture.* Minneapolis: Augsburg Fortress, 2011.